African History for Kids

A Captivating Guide to the

History of Africa

Table of Contents

INTRODUCTION

Africa is the second-largest continent on earth. It makes up 20 percent of the earth's landmass, which means there are many countries in Africa that all have their own rich histories to be unearthed! So, put your exploring cap on, and get ready to learn all about the history of this fascinating continent and its people.

Fun Fact: Africa is more than three times the size of the United States!

Throughout this book, you will explore the many kingdoms and empires of Africa from ancient times to today. Travel through the ancient Egyptian, Kush, and Aksum kingdoms before reaching medieval Africa. Then, be awed by the impressive Ghana, Kanem-Bornu, and Mali empires. You will discover the shocking truth about the horrific transatlantic slave trade and the colonization (settling with and controlling the indigenous/native peoples of an area) of Africa before finally learning how it all came to an end and how African countries regained their independence, which allows a (country to govern and control itself.

Watch history come alive with interesting images, fun facts, and amazing activities!

Chapter 1: Ancient Africa

Millions of years ago, Africa became the birthplace of human life. Many firsts for humanity took place on this continent. All the people of today are part of the species known as *Homo sapiens*, but before this, there were many other (now extinct) species of humans. One of the earliest types of humans was *Homo habilis*, who lived around 2.5 million years ago in the eastern and southern areas of Africa. *Homo habilis* were the first humans to use tools.

The discovery and ability to use fire was a vital step in the evolution of mankind. This was also made by early Africans approximately 1.4 million years ago.

Fun Fact: *Homo* is the Latin word for man.

The final step between the extinct *Homo erectus* species and modern-day *Homo sapiens* is also believed to have happened in Africa since the oldest fossils of modern man were found in Ethiopia.

Fun Fact: Africa is home to the oldest known examples of fishing, jewelry, math, animal domestication, crop cultivation, and more.

Seeing as it was the starting point for human life, it is perhaps no surprise that Africa was also home to one of the oldest human civilizations: Ancient Egypt. Ancient Egypt is estimated to have begun around 3150 BCE and ended in 30 BCE. It was centered around the Nile River on the northeastern coast of Africa. Before ancient Egypt began to flourish, there were only two other known homes to human civilizations: the Indus Valley (modern Afghanistan, Pakistan, and India) from 3300 BCE to 1900 BCE and the Mesopotamian civilizations (modern Iraq, Syria, and Turkey) from 3500 BCE to 500 BCE.

Many empires and kingdoms would follow ancient Egypt. Just below ancient Egypt, the Kingdom of Kush was established in 1070 BCE. Later, the neighboring Kingdom of Aksum would flourish. It was followed by the Ghana Empire, the Kanem-Bornu Empire, and the Mali Empire.

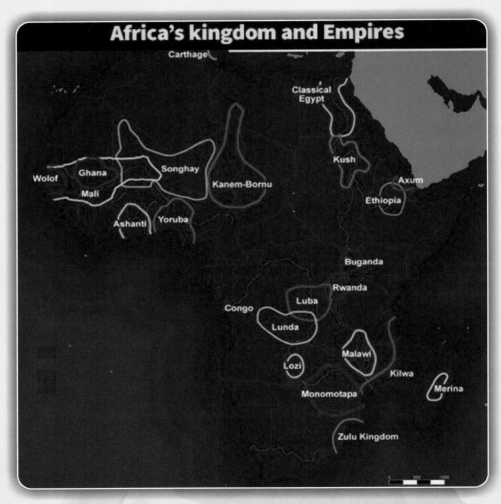

Map of the kingdoms of ancient Africa

Chapter 2: The Kingdom of Egypt

In this chapter, we're going to discover a little more information about the Kingdom of Egypt. We could fill a whole book on ancient Egypt (and we have—check out our *Ancient Egypt for Kids* book to learn more), but for now, we will just cover the main highlights of this important time in early African history.

The start of the ancient Egyptian civilization is known as the *Early Dynastic Period*. It was the start of Egypt being ruled by dynasties. A *dynasty* is a ruling family that passes leadership down through the family line.

Fun Fact: During the three thousand years of ancient Egypt, there were thirty different dynasties!

The first king of the Early Dynastic Period was *King Menes*. He was responsible for uniting Upper and Lower Egypt into one civilization and building the famous white-walled city of *Memphis*, which became the capital of ancient Egypt.

Map of the Early Dynastic Period of Egypt

Egypt is located in the northeast of Africa toward the top of the Nile River around the Nile Delta, where the river joins the Mediterranean Sea. One of the main reasons that the ancient Egyptian civilization was able to thrive was its access to the Nile River.

Fun Fact: The Nile is the longest river in the world, flowing 4,132 miles northward toward the Mediterranean Sea.

The Nile was not only a great source of drinking water. It was also vitally important for growing crops. Once a year, the river would flood, bringing in *silt*, a fine soil useful for planting and growing seeds. Without this yearly flooding, droughts could occur, causing widespread *famine* and starvation.

The unusual northward direction that the Nile flowed in was part of its success. Goods and building materials could be transported from the south. It was thanks to the Nile that the ancient Egyptians were able to build their impressive pyramids and monuments.

The first thing that likely comes to mind when thinking of Egypt is the pyramids. However, the first pyramids weren't built until five or six hundred years after the ancient Egyptian civilization began in the period known as the *Old Kingdom*. The most famous pyramid of all, *the Great Pyramid of Giza*, was built during this time by *King Khufu*.

Fun Fact: The Great Pyramid of Giza is one of the Seven Wonders of the Ancient World and can still be visited today!

The Great Pyramid was the first and largest pyramid (481 feet high) in the burial complex of Giza. The huge structure is made of 2.3 million stone blocks that weigh between 2.5 to 15 tons each! Historians are still unsure exactly how the Great Pyramid was built, but they estimate that between 20,000 to 100,000 people could have been involved!

Fun Fact: The Great Pyramid was built in just 23 years, meaning that 100,000 blocks a year, 285 blocks a day, or 1 block every 2 minutes had to be located, moved, prepared, and put in place! Phew, that sounds like a lot of work!

The Great Pyramid of Giza and the Sphinx (https://flic.kr/p/5JR1Dz)

Fun Fact: For almost 4,400 years, until the Eiffel Tower was built in 1889 in Paris, the Great Pyramid was the tallest structure on earth built by hand!

As well as building pyramids on the burial grounds, other monuments would also be built, such as *the Great Sphinx* in the Giza complex. A sphinx is a mythical creature with the head of a man and the body of a lion. The Great Sphinx was carved out of a single piece of limestone. It is an impressive 66-foot high and 240-foot-long construction, making it one of the biggest statues in the world!

In the burial complexes, there would also be grave markings known as *steles*. These large stone tablets would contain information about important people and events, which would be shown in *hieroglyphics*. Hieroglyphics was what the ancient Egyptians used for writing. It was a *pictorial* writing system. This means that they used pictures instead of letters, unlike the English alphabet.

Egyptian stele (https://flic.kr/p/XstBqa)

The most famous example of a stele ever discovered is the *Rosetta Stone*. The Rosetta Stone was accidentally discovered in 1799 CE by soldiers in Napoleon Bonaparte's army who were digging battle foundations near the Nile Delta. The Rosetta Stone was an incredibly important discovery. It helped historians finally *decipher* (understand and translate) Egyptian hieroglyphics. Since the language was no longer used, they could not read the hieroglyphics. However, the Rosetta Stone was written in three different languages, including hieroglyphics, so they could translate it based on the ancient Greek writing that was also on the stone.

Another type of structure still standing from ancient Egypt is the temples that were built to worship their many gods. These temples would be just as impressive as the pyramids. They often contained massive statues of pharaohs and gods, as well as huge stone columns.

An example of an Egyptian column
(https://flic.kr/p/XpJRPQ)

The ancient Egyptians built their impressive pyramids for a few reasons. First and foremost, they were used as burial grounds. But, of course, pyramids didn't need to be so large just to bury the dead. These huge monuments were created primarily due to their religious beliefs. They believed that to go on living in the afterlife, your name needed to be remembered by the living. Considering we are still talking about ancient Egypt and its kings, it's safe to say they achieved their goal of being remembered!

As well as King Menes and King Khufu, there were many other famous ancient Egyptian kings and pharaohs (pharaoh is another name for king and began to be used during the New Kingdom Period). Interestingly, one of the most famous pharaohs of all is also the most unlikely.

King Tutankhamun only ruled for ten years. He took the throne when he was only nine years old. When he died at the age of nineteen, he didn't leave behind a great monument to be remembered by. However, he became one of the most famous kings precisely because of his obscurity.

The tomb of King Tutankhamun was discovered in 1922 CE by *Howard Carter*, a British archaeologist. Many of the other bigger tombs in *the Valley of the Kings* were raided and their objects stolen years before modern historians found them. But because it was the smallest in the complex and the most hidden, King Tut's tomb remained undisturbed for over 3,200 years!

Fun Fact: Despite the tomb being the smallest in the Valley of the Kings, it still contained around five thousand artifacts! In fact, it took historians seventeen years to *catalog* (record) everything inside!

Among the artifacts in the tomb, the mummy of King Tutankhamun was also still there. It was perfectly preserved. Perhaps the most well-known artifact found inside the tomb was the blue and gold mask of the pharaoh.

Mask of Tutankhamun
https://commons.wikimedia.org/wiki/File:Tutmask.jpg

King Tutankhamun's mother-in-law, *Nefertiti*, is also very famous due to a well-preserved bust of her face that was discovered.

While King Tut didn't gain notoriety until thousands of years after his death, another very famous pharaoh of ancient Egypt, *Rameses II* (or Rameses the Great), is best remembered due to the enormous number of monuments built in his name. In fact, there is virtually no monument in Egypt that doesn't mention him!

Rameses II lived to be 96 years old. He ruled for so long that many of his subjects had never known another pharaoh, and they feared that when he died, the world would end!

Two other famous pharaohs often aren't thought of as being Egyptian rulers due to their Greek heritage. *Alexander the Great* conquered the *Persian Empire*, which had been in control of Egypt. This made him the new pharaoh. While he was in power, he created a new capital city, *Alexandria*. Although this city was Egyptian, it did not adopt only the Egyptian culture. In fact, it was very Greek in nature. It was here that *Cleopatra VII* was born. She was the last pharaoh of Egypt. Cleopatra is remembered for her beauty and her love affair with two powerful Greek rulers, *Julius Caesar* and *Mark Antony*.

If you'd like to learn more about ancient Egypt, including more details on their pharaohs, what life was like, their religious beliefs, and why they mummified the dead, check out our *Ancient Egypt for Kids* guide!

Chapter 2 Activities

1. Who was King Menes? What did he do?

2. Where is Egypt located?

3. Why was the Nile so important?

4. What is a sphinx?

5. Why was the Rosetta Stone important?

Chapter 2 Answers

1. King Menes was the first ruler of ancient Egypt. He united Upper and Lower Egypt and built the capital city of Memphis.

2. Egypt is located in the northeast of Africa toward the top of the Nile River, where the river joins the Mediterranean Sea.

3. The Nile was vital to the Egyptian civilization since it provided drinking water and water for crops. It was also used to transport goods and stone for building cities and monuments.

4. A sphinx is a mythical creature with the head of a man and the body of a lion. Fun

    Fact: Both Greek and Asian mythology adopted the sphinx. Both of these versions had wings.

5. The Rosetta Stone was important since it helped historians finally read hieroglyphics.

Chapter 3: The Kingdom of Kush

Our next ancient African kingdom is the Kingdom of Kush, which is also often referred to as *Nubia*. Nubia was located just below Egypt to the south. The two kingdoms had many ties and similarities. Kush and its capital cities were located around the Nile River, White River, and Blue River. Today, the country of Sudan is where Kush used to be.

Before it gained its independence in 1070 BCE, Kush was part of Egypt. But with the decline of the New Kingdom of Egypt around that time, Kush was able to break free of Egyptian rule and establish its own kingdom. The city-state of *Napata* became its capital.

Fun Fact: Nubia was often nicknamed the "Land of the Bow" because the bow and arrow was their weapon of choice in battle.

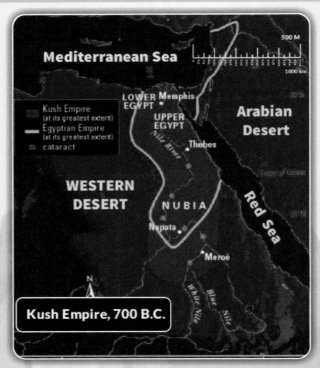

Map of ancient Kush, ancient Egypt, and the surrounding areas.

In 746 BCE, the *Kushites* managed to conquer Egypt under the rule of *King Piye*. This began the 25th Dynasty of Egypt. Egypt remained under Kushite control until 653 BCE, when they were driven out by the *Assyrians*.

Fun Fact: The Assyrians and later rulers of Egypt tried to erase the evidence of Kushite rule by destroying many of their statues and steles.

The final era of the Kingdom of Kush is often referred to as the *Meroitic Period*. The Meroitic Period began in 300 BCE and continued until the Kingdom of Kush became part of the *Kingdom of Aksum* in 330 CE. During this time, the capital city of Kush became *Meroë*. Meroë was a port city located on the Nile River. It was useful as a trade route to other areas. Not only was the soil good for crops there, but it was also very close to iron and gold mines. These were the main sources of wealth for the Kingdom of Kush.

There were many similarities between the Kushite and Egyptian cultures. The Kushites believed in the Egyptian gods. They built pyramids and mummified their dead. The Kushite pyramids were smaller than the Egyptian ones. They were no taller than 98 feet high, and their bases were around 22 feet wide. To put that into perspective, the Great Pyramid of Giza is four times taller and has a base of 756 feet! The Kushite pyramids were also far steeper than their Egyptian counterparts, with an incline of seventy degrees compared to the fifty-degree angle of the Egyptian ones.

Fun Fact: Although the Kushite pyramids may have been smaller, there were more pyramids in one burial complex in Meroë than in the whole of Egypt!

The pyramids of Meroë. Credit: Christopher Michel, Flickr.

(https://flic.kr/p/S55wS4   https://flic.kr/p/QQ4X6B)

Like many ancient civilizations, religion was a very important part of the daily life and culture of Kush. The Kushites adopted many of the Egyptian gods as their own. The main god they worshiped was *Amun*, who was often depicted as a man with the head of a ram or as a ram. Amun was a creator god and the god of the sun and air. Amun was less clearly defined than other gods. His name roughly means "hidden one" or "invisible." Because of this, the people could define him as what they needed him to be.

An important Kushite deity was *Apedemak*, who was the god of war. He had the head of a lion. His wife, *Amesemi*, was a protective goddess who wore a falcon-shaped crown.

Like ancient Egypt, the Kingdom of Kush was based on a class system. At the top were the king and priests. The priests were so powerful that they decided who would become king and when the king died. If they believed the king was no longer a suitable ruler, they would tell him that the god Amun had decided that it was time for him to die.

The classes below the ruler and priests were the artisans and scribes. The artisans were responsible for making items out of gold and iron. These were the two most important goods that Kush exported and used. Iron was used to make strong weapons and tools. Gold provided wealth and would often be traded with their Egyptian neighbors. The next class was made up of the farmers. The large majority of Kushites were farmers, and they mainly grew barley and wheat or cotton to make clothes. Finally, the lowest social class was made up of slaves and servants.

Although the Kushite culture was similar to the Egyptians, they had many differences. After the 1st century BCE, the ruler, *Arkamani*, decided that Kush needed to move away from the Egyptian culture and embrace their own. He ended the priests' power over the throne and encouraged the worship of Kushite gods. He also discarded the Egyptian hieroglyphic writing in favor of a new Kushite language, *Meroitic*.

Fun Fact: To this day, the Meroitic language has still not been deciphered.

Arkamani also introduced queens, known as *Kandakes* or *Candaces*, to Kush. The throne would be passed down *matrilineally*. This means the family would be traced through the female line.

The Kushites also looked different from their Egyptian neighbors. In Egyptian artwork, the Kushites are shown to have darker skin and shorter hair. The Kushites also wore different clothing, favoring patterned material, animal skins, and big earrings.

Artifacts from the Kingdom of Kush
(https://flic.kr/p/Wygoka)

Chapter 3 Activities

1. Where was the Kingdom of Kush located?

2. What other name is sometimes used to describe the Kingdom of Kush?

3. Did the Kushite culture and customs resemble any other culture?

4. What weapon did the Kushite soldiers famously use?

5. What were the main sources of wealth for Kush?

Chapter 3 Answers

1. The Kingdom of Kush was located to the south of Egypt around the Nile River, White River, and Blue River in what is now the country of Sudan.

2. The Kingdom of Kush is also sometimes called Nubia.

3. The Kushite culture and customs strongly resembled the Egyptians.

4. The Kushite soldiers famously used bows and arrows for weapons.

5. Their main sources of wealth were gold and iron.

Chapter 4: The Kingdom of Aksum

The Kingdom of Aksum, also referred to as Axum, was located in East Africa in the area known as the Horn of Africa by the Red Sea. As well as covering the northern part of modern-day Ethiopia, it also covered parts of other countries, such as Eritrea, Sudan, Yemen, and Saudi Arabia.

Fun Fact: The city of Axum still exists in Ethiopia today. It is one of the oldest continually occupied cities in Africa.

Map of the Kingdom of Aksum.

According to legend, the Kingdom of Aksum was founded by the son of *King Solomon* and the *Queen of Sheba*. King Solomon was the king of Israel. He appears in the Hebrew Bible, the Christian Old Testament, and the Islamic Quran. King Solomon is depicted as a wise ruler. Perhaps the most well-known story of his wisdom is the one in which two mothers came to him. They both claimed that a baby was theirs. King Solomon tricked the women by saying that the solution was to cut the baby in half. Solomon knew that the real mother would give up her child to the other woman since she would do anything to save it. One of the women agreed to the solution, so he was able to determine who the real mother was and return the baby to her unharmed. It is because of his wisdom that the Queen of Sheba reportedly decided to visit King Solomon.

While King Solomon can be traced back to a real ruler, there is no evidence other than the biblical stories that the Queen of Sheba existed. But, according to legend, she was from the Aksum area. The gifts of gold, spices, and precious gems she brought with her also help support this theory, as these can all be found in the Horn of Africa. It is said that while she was visiting Solomon, the Queen of Sheba fell pregnant with his son, *Menelik*. He was raised as a Jew and eventually founded the *Solomonic Dynasty*. Later, Aksum would go on to embrace Christianity, but many Ethiopian Jews refused to adopt Christianity and still practice Judaism to this day.

King Menelik would eventually go and meet his father, Solomon. It is rumored that the son of a high priest, *Azariah*, went to Aksum with Menelik. He stole the *Ark of the Covenant* and brought it to Aksum with him. King Solomon began to chase after Azariah when he discovered it was missing. However, he had a dream that it needed to be with his son. So, he returned to Jerusalem and commanded his priests to keep its disappearance a secret.

Fun Fact: The Ark of the Covenant is believed to contain the two stone tablets that the Ten Commandments are written on. The sacred object is said to be a wooden box covered in gold with two golden *cherubim* (cherubs or angels) on top called the *mercy seat*.

But let's look at the real facts instead of legends. We know the Kingdom of Aksum didn't become more powerful until around 100 CE. We don't know whether the kingdom was a different one from what Menelik ruled. This is because the early records of Aksum are scarce.

Aksum became powerful because it had control over major points of trade. They were also successful in their farming efforts due to the rich soil and reliable rainy season. Aksum was connected to many trade routes, including the Nile River, the Red Sea, and the Gulf of Aden. The main trade city was *Adulis*. All sorts of desirable objects and necessary items were exchanged here. The Aksum people would trade ivory and gold with India and the Mediterranean. The Romans would trade olive oil or wine. The Indians had spices and jewels to offer. The Aksumites also grew wheat and barley, which they would trade.

Fun Fact: Because of traders coming from all over the world to Aksum, Greek was the most commonly used language by merchants.

While Greek was commonly used, the Aksumites also had their own language, *Ge'ez*. Ge'ez was written in the *boustrophedon* style. This means it was written from left to right. The next line would be from right to left, and it would continue to alternate the direction of each line. The oldest version of the language did not have vowels. However, when Christianity was introduced, vowels were also introduced. This happened because it allowed the people to convert the Bible into Ge'ez more easily.

Coin of the Aksumite King Ezana
(https://commons.wikimedia.org/wiki/File:Endubis.jpg#/media/File:Endubis.jpg)

Because of their strong trading culture, the Aksumites also minted their own coins. These were made from gold, silver, or copper. They were one of the few ancient kingdoms to have done this. Gold coins were usually used for foreign trade. They would be inscribed with Greek. The silver and copper coins would have Ge'ez on them. The first Aksumite coins were similar in design and weight to the Roman ones. They depicted the ruling king, *King Endubis*, religious symbols of the sun and moon, and a type of wheat called *teff*.

When *King Ezana* was in power, he decided to change the symbols on the coins to contain a cross. This demonstrates the religious change to Christianity that had taken place. King Ezana is thought to have become king sometime between 320 and 325. It is rumored that he converted to Christianity because of a former slave and tutor of his, *Frumentius*. Aksum became the first Christian state in Africa, and it was one of the first states in the world to make it the state religion. Ezana may have been influenced to convert due to a desire to strengthen trade deals with the Romans. A stele called the *Ezana Stone* depicts King Ezana's conversion and conquest of nearby areas, such as Meroë. The Ezana Stone has been compared to the Rosetta Stone because it is also written in three different languages. The three languages on the Ezana Stone are Ge'ez, Greek, and *Sabaean*.

The Ezana Stone. Credit: Wikimedia Commons, Sailko

The Ezana Stone and many other steles were found in the town of Aksum near the Church of Our Lady Mary of Zion. This is where the Ark of the Covenant is rumored to be hidden. The steles are sometimes referred to as *obelisks*. These are tall stone monuments that are *monolithic*. This means they were carved from a single piece of stone. One of the steles here, known as the Great Stele (also spelled as Great Stela), is likely to have been the biggest monolith ever attempted. However, because of its massive 520-ton weight, it fell during construction.

The Obelisk of Aksum weighs less than half of the Great Stele. It is about 160 tons and is almost 80 feet tall. Just like its bigger counterpart, the Obelisk of Aksum also fell at some point. In 1937, invading Italian soldiers removed the obelisk, and it was taken back to Rome, where it was re-erected. They had to cut the obelisk into three since it was so big! Despite a United Nations ruling in 1947 that said it should be returned to Ethiopia, the stele remained in Rome for seventy years. It was returned in 2005.

Fun Fact: In 2008, 1,700 years after it was first built, the monument was once again erected in the same place.

The third-largest stele was built to honor King Ezana. It is the largest unbroken stele left standing. It is thought to be the last one built, as the shift to Christianity meant that steles were no longer used as burial markers.

The Obelisk of Aksum
(https://commons.wikimedia.org/wiki/File:Salt_and_Havell_(1809)
_The_Obelisk_at_Axum.png#/media/File:Salt_and_Havell_(1809)_The_Obelisk_at_Axum.png)

The Kingdom of Aksum reached its peak during King Ezana's rule. It thrived until 960. According to legend, it was conquered by a foreign queen. However, many factors led to the ultimate downfall of the Kingdom of Aksum. Perhaps most crucially was the loss of its trade routes during wars against the Islamic armies. The once fertile soil they used for crops also began to dry out, and the *Justinian Plague* killed many of the Aksum people.

Fun Fact: The Justinian Plague was the first known occurrence of the bubonic plague. It may have been responsible for as many as fifty million deaths!

Chapter 4 Activities

1. What is another common name for the Kingdom of Aksum?

   A) Egypt   B) Axum   C) Kush

2. Who is thought to have first established Aksum?

   A) King Menes   B) King Ezana

   C) King Menelik, the son of King Solomon

3. What leader converted the kingdom to Christianity?

   A) King Ezana   B) King Solomon   C) Queen Cleopatra

4. What type of structure was Aksum famous for constructing?

   A) Pyramids   B) Monuments   C) Tall towers called steles

5. As well as their own language of Ge'ez, what other language was common?

   A) Latin   B) Greek   C) Arabic

Chapter 4 Answers

1. What is another common name for the Kingdom of Aksum?

   A) Axum

2. Who is thought to have first established Aksum?

   B) King Menelik, the son of King Solomon

3. What leader converted the kingdom to Christianity?

   A) King Ezana

4. What type of structure was Aksum famous for constructing?

   C) Tall towers called steles

5. As well as their own language of Ge'ez, what other language was common?

   B) Greek

Chapter 5: Medieval Africa

Many people mistakenly believe that Africa is a "dark continent" without much history, especially during the medieval period. However, this was not the case. The thousand-year medieval period (500 to 1500 CE) was a time of cultural, religious, and economic growth in Africa.

Fun Fact: It is estimated that Africa may have had up to ten thousand different states during the medieval period, each with its own language and culture!

At the start of the medieval period, Egypt had been under Roman rule since 30 CE. As well as introducing different cultures and using Egypt for trade, the Romans also introduced Christianity to the continent. After many years of fighting off Arab armies, the Romans eventually lost Egypt to them in 646. The new Arabic armies also brought their own religion: Islam.

During this time, the *Ghana Empire* was established, and new trade routes began to emerge around the Indian Ocean. The main items traded were slaves, gold, salt, and ivory. The demand for gold and salt was so high that a completely new trade route through the Sahara Desert was created. Before this, the Sahara Desert had been avoided due to its harsh climate. Because of the new trade route, new kingdoms emerged in this area in 700. These new states made trade even easier via this route.

From 500 to 1250 CE, ancient Ghana flourished as an organized society. It had a matrilineal monarchy and a system of law and order. It was reasonably wealthy due to its trade routes.

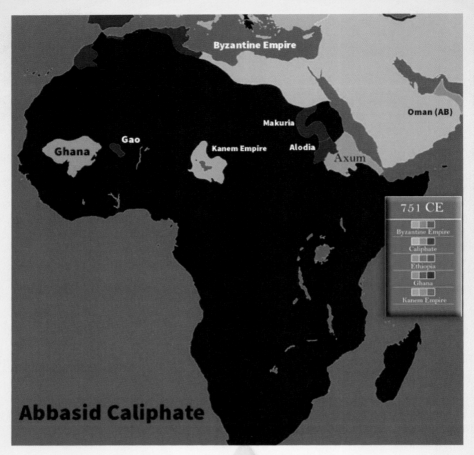

Map of medieval Africa, 751.

The next major kingdom during the medieval Africa period was the Kanem-Bornu Empire, which ran from the 9th century to the 19th century.

The *Mali Empire* began in 1235. It was in the same area as Ghana had been but went even farther along the *Niger River*. Most of the people in Mali lived in small villages. They worked as farmers or fishermen. Trade also flourished during this time, and Islam grew as a religion. Mali would have a *Mansa* as their ruler. He was chosen to rule by a council of leaders.

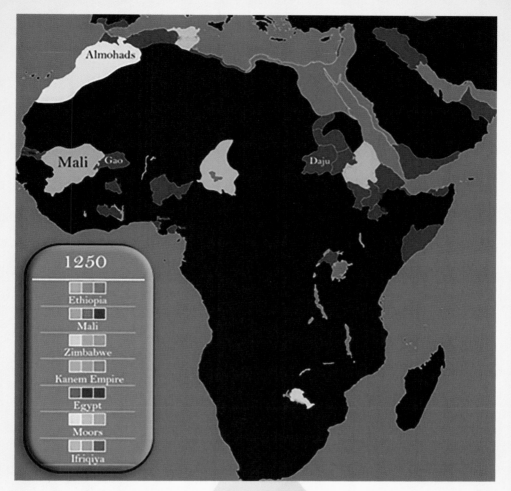

Map of medieval Africa, 1250

Around 1375, the state of *Gao*, which was based around a *tributary* (small stream or river that flows into a larger one) in Mali, broke away from Mali rule. This became the *Songhai Empire*.

Fun Fact: The leader of the Songhai Empire, *Sunni Ali*, managed to turn a very small town into a huge empire in just 28 years!

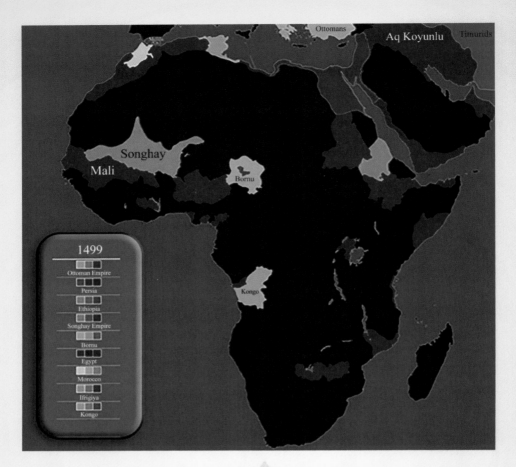

Map of medieval Africa, 1499

Because of the increased trade going on during the medieval period, African architecture began to flourish, as they were now rich enough to build with stone. In addition to building city walls, palaces, and houses, impressive churches and mosques were also built. In other, less affluent areas of Africa, buildings would be made from mudbrick.

Fun Fact: While Islam and Christianity were both growing in popularity in Africa throughout the Middle Ages, Christianity remained the major religion in Europe.

The Islamic people who had overthrown the Romans in North Africa decided to move away from the existing cities and start fresh. They built new cities nearby. Mosques dominated the cities. The capital of Egypt—Alexandria—moved and became *Fustat*, which is now called Cairo. Carthage moved to Tunisia, and a new city, *Kairouan*, was built in the desert there. Kairouan went on to be known as the fourth holiest city of Islam.

Fun Fact: The top three holiest cities of Islam are Mecca, Medina, and Jerusalem.

One of the most important buildings in Kairouan was the Great Mosque. It was built around 800 CE during the *Abbasid Caliphate*. A caliphate is similar to an empire. It is used to distinguish the states under Islamic rule. The Great Mosque was very impressive and far grander than anything being built in Europe at the time.

The Great Mosque of Kairouan, 670. Credit: Marek Szarejko, Wikimedia Commons
(https://commons.wikimedia.org/wiki/File:Great_Mosque_of_Kairouan_Panorama_-_Grande_
Mosqu%C3%A9e_de_Kairouan_Panorama.jpg#/media/File:Great_Mosque_of_Kairouan_
Panorama_-_Grande_Mosquée_de_Kairouan_Panorama.jpg)

The Great Mosque had several stone columns that were taken from existing Roman buildings. They decided to use the old columns rather than build new ones. They likely felt this move was symbolic of the Islamic defeat of the Romans.

At the Great Mosque, a *minaret* was also built. A minaret is a tower with stairs and an opening at the top. Islamic holy men would climb the minaret five times a day to announce the call to prayer (*muezzin*).

Fun Fact: The minaret at Kairouan was built in 700 CE. It is the oldest minaret still standing in the world!

Another impressive mosque built in this period was *the Great Mosque of Kilwa Kisiwani*. It was built during the 11th century. Kilwa Kisiwani is an island off the coast of Tanzania. At this time, Kilwa was a major port. It was vitally important to the success of the Indian Ocean trade route. Today, Kilwa Kisiwani is a UNESCO World Heritage Site.

Fun Fact: After the decline of Aksum, Kilwa was the first place south of the Sahara to mint gold coins.

The buildings at Kilwa Kisiwani were made from fossil coral limestone. For more decorative parts, they would use *porites*, a type of living stone-like coral. Mollusk shells, coral, and limestone would be crushed and combined with water to create white paint. When mixed with dirt or sand, this created a type of *mortar*.

The Great Mosque of Kilwa Kisiwani is an important part of African history. It is the oldest surviving mosque on the eastern coast of Africa. It is also one of the first mosques to have been built without a courtyard.

Fun Fact: While most mosques often only have one dome, the Great Mosque of Kilwa has an impressive sixteen domes!

The Great Mosque of Kilwa Kisiwani. Credit: Ron Van Oers, Wikimedia Commons
(https://commons.wikimedia.org/wiki/File:Ruins_of_Kilwa_Kisiwani_and_Ruins_of_Songo_Mnara-
108279.jpg#/media/File:Ruins_of_Kilwa_Kisiwani_and_Ruins_of_Songo_Mnara-108279.jpg ;
https://commons.wikimedia.org/wiki/File:Inside_the_great_mosque_of_
Kilwa.jpg#/media/File:Inside_the_great_mosque_of_Kilwa.jpg)

Inside the Great Mosque of Kilwa Kisiwani. Credit: Robin Chew, Wikimedia Commons
(https://commons.wikimedia.org/wiki/File:Inside_the_great_mosque_
of_Kilwa.jpg#/media/File:Inside_the_great_mosque_of_Kilwa.jpg)

Another empire known for its architecture during this time was the *Ajuran Empire*. It was located in the Horn of Africa. The Ajuran Empire was predominantly Muslim and had a *theocratic* (religious) government. Many mosques were established throughout this empire, and most people converted to Islam. They also built many fortresses and castles.

Under the Ajuran *Sultanate* (a country run by a *sultan*), the small town of *Mogadishu* became the religious center of the empire. The wealthy and metropolitan city of Mogadishu was famous for its fine fabrics, which its merchants would trade all over the world via the Indian Ocean.

Fun Fact: Zheng He, a Chinese naval officer, was the first Chinese person to officially visit Africa. He went on a number of missions there during the 15th century, including to Mogadishu. He brought back the first African animals to China. The sultan of Mogadishu later visited and set up an embassy in China.

Just under twenty miles off the coast of Mogadishu is a small island in the Somali Sea. It contains many ruins that are typical of Ajuran architecture. One of these is the *Citadel* (fortress) of *Gondershe*.

The Citadel of Gondershe, Somalia
(https://commons.wikimedia.org/wiki/File:Gondereshe2008.jpg#/media/File:Gondereshe2008.jpg)

There were also many technological advancements during the Middle Ages in Africa. *Astronomy* (the scientific study of *celestial* objects in space) had been studied in Africa since the ancient Egyptians. Some significant discoveries happened in astronomy during the 12th to 16th centuries in Timbuktu.

One thing they believed in was *heliocentrism*. This means they thought the earth and other planets revolved around the sun. Many parts of the world at this time, especially Europe, believed that the opposite was true. They thought that the earth was the center of the universe, with the sun and other planets orbiting it.

They also used the *Julian calendar*, a calendar that was created by Julius Caesar. It is practically the same as the calendar still used in the Western world today. The main difference is that the Julian calendar had a leap year every three years. The one used today has a leap year every four years.

They also created impressive mathematical diagrams of the solar system, recorded astrological events, such as meteor showers, and calculated their exact location in relation to Mecca.

Fun Fact: Today, South Africa has many astronomers. It is home to the largest optical telescope in the Southern Hemisphere.

Africa also made medical advancements during the medieval period. Around the year 800 CE, the first hospital that specialized in caring for the mentally ill was built in Egypt. One would also be built in Baghdad around this time. The first mental asylum in Europe didn't open until 1247 in London. Not long after this, in 1285, Egypt went on to open the biggest hospital of the medieval period. Treatment was free to everyone. National healthcare was not established in Europe until 1948.

Fun Fact: In 1100 CE, the ventilator was invented in Egypt.

Chapter 5 Activities

Draw a line to connect the fact to its corresponding answer.

How often does the Julian calendar have a leap year?	The Arabs
Domes are a common feature in which type of building?	Europe
Zheng He took giraffes, hippos, ostriches, and more back to what country?	Mosques
The first psychological hospital was in what country?	Egypt
Christianity was the only dominant religion here during the Middle Ages.	3 years
Which people brought Islam to Africa?	China
What buildings do Christians worship in?	Churches

Chapter 5 Answers

Draw a line to connect the fact to its corresponding answer.

How often does the Julian calendar have a leap year?	3 years
Domes are a common feature in which type of building?	Mosques
Zheng He took giraffes, hippos, ostriches, and more back to what country?	China
The first psychological hospital was in what country?	Egypt
Christianity was the only dominant religion here during the Middle Ages.	Europe
Which people brought Islam to Africa?	The Arabs
What buildings do Christians worship in?	Churches

Chapter 6: The Ghana Empire

Now, we are going to learn more about the medieval African empires. First up is the *Ghana Empire*. It ran from approximately 300 to 1240 CE. The Ghana Empire was founded by several different tribes known as the *Soninke* people. They were united under the rule of the empire's first king, *Dinga Cisse*.

Fun Fact: The Ghana Empire is not to be confused with the modern-day Republic of Ghana, which is located in a different part of Africa. They are not related culturally.

The Ghana Empire was located in the west of Africa, where modern-day Mali, Senegal, and Mauritania now exist. Trade and transportation were made possible to the Ghana Empire thanks to the three main rivers in the area: the Niger River, Gambia River, and Senegal River.

Map of the Ghana Empire at its greatest extent.

Fun Fact: To travel to the Ghana Empire from the coast, you had to cross the Sahara Desert on camelback—this would take forty days on average!

Fun Fact: The Ghana Empire was actually referred to as *Wagadu* by its rulers. "Ghana" actually came from their word for king, *ghāna*.

The Ghana Empire was made up of several villages that were all under the rule of the ghāna. The ghāna was in control of many things, including the empire's justice system and religion. The people practiced *animism*. They believed that everything had a spiritual element and was alive. This included humans, animals, plants, rocks, weather, rivers, and so on. All of these elements were believed to have a direct interest in the lives of humans. They could help or hinder them. As the leader of this religion, the ghāna was treated with reverence. Sacrifices were made in his honor. When the ghāna died, he was buried on sacred land, which no one was allowed to enter.

During the Middle Ages, Islam became increasingly popular throughout Africa due to merchants from Arabic countries introducing Islam to the continent. However, the ghānas of the Ghana Empire did not convert to Islam.

While they did not fully convert to Islam, those who believed in the native religion and those who converted to Islam lived alongside each other. The capital city, *Koumbi Saleh*, was split in half. One side was Muslim, while the other believed in animism. The Muslim side of the city housed twelve mosques. Just over six miles away, on the other side of the capital, there was the palace and traditional shrines. This suggests that these two religions lived side by side in relative harmony.

When the ruins of Koumbi Saleh were discovered in 1913 by French archaeologists, they discovered a number of important artifacts, including *epigraphic shale plates* (a type of rock made into tablets with writing on them). These had religious inscriptions and geometric patterns on them.

Epigraphic shale plate from Koumbi Saleh. Credit: Clemens Schmillen, Wikimedia Commons

(https://commons.wikimedia.org/wiki/File:NouakchottNational Museum2.jpg#/media/File:NouakchottNationalMuseum2.jpg)

Another famous town in the Ghana Empire was *Chinguetti*. Like Koumbi Saleh, Chinguetti is now a UNESCO World Heritage Site. It has many fascinating ruins. The town was at the center of many of the trade routes. These trade routes helped the Ghana Empire grow to become powerful and wealthy.

In Chinguetti, the buildings are constructed from mudbrick and a reddish dry stone. The flat roofs were made from palm, while the doors were hand-cut from giant *acacia trees*. As well as a mosque, the town also had a fortress and a water tower. Chinguetti was home to five libraries that contained scientific and religious Islamic texts that date as far back as the Middle Ages.

Chinguetti, a town that was part of the Ghana Empire
(https://commons.wikimedia.org/wiki/File:Chinguetti-Vue_Goblale_Vieille_
ville.jpg#/media/File:Chinguetti-Vue_Goblale_Vieille_ville.jpg)

Fun Fact: The Ghana Empire was often nicknamed the "Land of Gold."

The rulers of the Ghana Empire also had control over the empire's immense wealth. One of the main trading commodities that the Ghana Empire possessed was its vast amount of gold.

Fun Fact: The ghāna stockpiled gold nuggets and forbade anyone from owning gold. Merchants were only permitted gold dust.

Forbidding others from owning gold nuggets meant that the ghāna could control the value of gold and make sure it didn't go down. If there was too much gold available at any given time, it would not be as valuable or desirable.

As well as an abundance of gold, the Ghana Empire also traded in other local resources. This included copper, ivory, and iron. Iron was used to create strong weapons and tools for their army.

Fun Fact: Metalworkers who made iron were considered to be magical since they used fire and earth to create something new.

Another desirable and highly valued commodity of the time was salt. Slaves would mine the salt from the Sahara Desert. If anyone wanted to trade salt, it would be subject to very high taxes. Salt was so valuable it could even be used as currency.

Fun Fact: Salt was worth the same as gold!

The decline of the Ghana Empire began for several reasons. Climate change factored in when unusually dry weather occurred. Also, new trade routes that were farther east and easier for merchants to get to began to become more popular, cutting off their once-lucrative trade deals.

On top of this, a group of Muslim *Berber* tribes known as the *Almoravids* began a holy crusade to convert people to Islam. When the rulers of the Ghana Empire refused to convert, civil wars broke out between the two religions. This led to economic instability. Many tribal chiefs took advantage of the chaos and established independent kingdoms.

Over a period of hundreds of years, the Ghana Empire began to disintegrate. In 1240, it became part of the Mali Empire.

Chapter 6 Activities

True or false?

1. The Ghana Empire was founded by Emperor Mansa.

2. The capital of the Kingdom of Ghana was Koumbi Saleh.

3. Dinga Cisse was the first king of the newly formed empire.

4. After its fall, the Ghana Empire became a part of the Kanem-Bornu Empire.

5. Only the king was allowed to own gold nuggets.

6. The Ghana Empire would take one hundred days to reach on camelback from the coast. There was only one religion in the Ghana Empire.

7. The Ghana Empire was actually referred to as Wagadu.

Chapter 6 Answers

True or false?

1. **The Ghana Empire was founded by Emperor Mansa. — False**

   It was founded when a group of tribes united under King Dinga Cisse.

2. **The capital of the Kingdom of Ghana was Koumbi Saleh. — True**

3. **Dinga Cisse was the first king of the newly formed empire. — True**

4. **After its fall, the Ghana Empire became a part of the Kanem-Bornu Empire. — False**

   It became part of the Mali Empire.

5. **Only the king was allowed to own gold nuggets. — True**

6. **The Ghana Empire would take one hundred days to reach on camelback from the coast. — False**

   On average, it took forty days.

7. **There was only one religion in the Ghana Empire. — False**

   Islam and animism were the two main religions.

8. **The Ghana Empire was actually referred to as Wagadu. — True**

Chapter 7: The Kanem-Bornu Empire

Our journey through African history has now led us to the time when the *Kanem-Bornu Empire* reigned supreme. The Kanem-Bornu Empire was based around *Lake Chad*. It spanned modern-day Chad, Nigeria, Cameroon, Niger, and Libya.

Fun Fact: When it was first founded, it was known as the Kanem Empire. Bornu was added later.

Around 700 CE, *Kanem* was settled by the previously nomadic *Zaghawa* or *Kanembu* people. Its first ruling family was from the *Duguwa Dynasty*. However, the Kanembu people did not discover Kanem. It was already occupied by the *Sao culture*. Historians think the Sao civilization could have been there since as early as 600 BCE.

Fun Fact: The occupation was not amicable. A civil war went on between the Sao and Kanembu people until the 16th century.

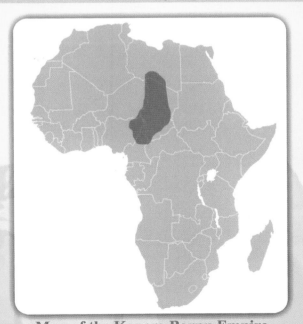

Map of the Kanem-Bornu Empire

(https://commons.wikimedia.org/wiki/File:Kanem-Bornu.svg)

The existing walled cities built by the Sao and fertile lands were the main reasons that the Kanembu decided to settle in Kanem. They created a new city, *N'jimi* (which meant "south"). This city became the capital.

In 1023, the Kanem Empire expanded into the Sahara Desert under the rule of *King Arku*. By taking over this area, they also gained control of the trade routes. This trade provided the empire with wealth. It also meant that the people of Kanem were introduced to Islam.

Fun Fact: The main items that the Kanembu people traded were slaves, ostrich feathers, and ivory.

The next *mai* (ruler) was important for two reasons. Firstly, this might have been the first female queen of the empire. However, it is not known for sure if this particular ruler was male or female. More importantly, this was the first mai to convert to Islam. This ruler was known as Hu or Hawwa. They only reigned for four years (1067-1071). Their successors were also Muslim.

After over three hundred years of the Duguwa Dynasty, a new dynasty appeared. This was the *Sefuwa Dynasty*. It was formed around 1075. The Sefuwa Dynasty was one of the longest in African history. It ran until 1846. It was one of the most important Muslim kingdoms in Africa during this period.

The Sefuwa Dynasty not only had its own land. It was also in charge of twelve other states. On top of expanding the empire, the Sefuwa Dynasty also managed to gain control of the valuable salt mines in Bilma. They would use the salt to trade for glass, horses, and fabric. The horses they traded for were especially vital for the expansion of the empire. This was because their soldiers would ride into battle on horseback. *Mai Dunama Dibalami* was responsible for further expanding the empire during his reign. He ruled from 1210 until 1248.

This expansion was largely thanks to his army of forty thousand men and horses.

A group of Kanem warriors

(https://commons.wikimedia.org/wiki/File:Group_of_Kanem-Bu_warriors.jpg)

At the start of 1500, Kanem became known as Kanem-Bornu. This is because, in the 14th century, the *Bulala people* of Chad forced the *mai* to abandon the capital and move it to an area called *Bornu*. Fortunately, the move to Bornu was successful. It was more fertile there. This led to new trade deals with the *Hausa Kingdoms* in modern-day Nigeria. By 1497, *Mai Ali Ghaji* was powerful enough to recapture Kanem, and the kingdom began to be known as the Kanem-Bornu Empire.

Fun Fact: The Kanem-Bornu Empire wasn't officially known as this until 1617, when the Kanem and Bornu regions were unified.

Mai Idris Alooma ruled from 1564 to 1596. He was one of the most successful mais and was known for his military prowess. He reportedly fought and won over 1,000 battles and 330 wars. He came up with new military tactics, such as building walls around battle camps, using armor for soldiers and horses, and *scorched-earth tactics*. This means the soldiers destroyed anything that the enemy needed, such as land, housing, and food. He also introduced camels from the Sahara to replace the less suitable oxen and donkeys that were being used.

Idris Alooma was a devout Muslim. He went on a *pilgrimage* (a spiritual journey) in 1571 to the Islamic holy land, Mecca. He encouraged his people to do the same. He also improved the justice system by appointing qualified officials to uphold the law.

The Kanem-Bornu Empire did not last long once the Sefuwa Dynasty ended. In 1893, the empire was overthrown by *Rabih az-Zubayr* from Sudan. He did not remain in control of the empire for long. European forces soon arrived, and the land was divided and conquered.

A depiction of a young woman from Bornu

(https://commons.wikimedia.org/wiki/File:Young_woman_from_Bornu.jpg)

The rulers and noblemen would wear wool and cotton. The people of Kanem-Bornu would mostly wear clothing made from crocodile or leopard skin.

In the Kanem-Bornu Empire, people had jobs that were similar to those elsewhere in Africa. The lower-class people would be slaves, soldiers, or farmers. Farming was considered an important job, and the workers were paid. They would grow wheat, beans, and a common type of ancient grain called *millet*. Artisans and merchants were also important jobs since they helped grow the wealth of the kingdom and traded for valuable goods.

The highest position for noblemen was to be in the government. The mai would ask them for help when making any decisions.

Fun Fact: The two highest positions in the government were held by women—the queen mother and queen sister.

The Kanem-Bornu Empire was made up of many different states. They all had their own unique customs, but they shared the same religion, language, and culture. Some cities were so big that they became capitals themselves. They would be in control of hundreds of nearby villages. Each city-state was controlled by a council of important members of society. This included the rulers, the head of the police, and the chief of finance.

Fun Fact: The biggest city-states were home to over 100,000 people at their peak.

The flag of the Bornu Empire
(https://commons.wikimedia.org/wiki/File:Flag_of_the_Bornu_
Empire.svg#/media/File:Flag_of_the_Bornu_Empire.svg)

Chapter 7 Activities

Oh, no! The timeline of the Kanem-Bornu Empire is all jumbled up below. Can you reorder the events correctly?

1. The reign of King Idris Alooma began.

2. The empire was founded by the Zaghawa or Kanembu nomadic people.

3. The Kanem Empire expanded into the Sahara.

4. The Kanem-Bornu Empire was taken over by Sudan.

5. Bornu recaptured the lost territories and became the Kanem-Bornu Empire.

6. Islam was adopted as the state religion.

7. The Sefuwa Dynasty began.

Chapter 7 Answers

1. The empire was founded by the Zaghawa or Kanembu nomadic people.

2. The Kanem Empire expanded into the Sahara.

3. Islam was adopted as the state religion.

4. The Sefuwa Dynasty began.

5. Bornu recaptured the lost territories and became the Kanem-Bornu Empire.

6. The reign of King Idris Alooma began.

7. The Kanem-Bornu Empire was taken over by Sudan.

Chapter 8: The Mali Empire

We are going to learn more about another medieval African empire. This one is the *Mali Empire*. It was formed around 1235 CE by *Sundiata Keita*. He united lots of smaller *Malinké* kingdoms that were located in the west of Africa around the Niger River.

Fun Fact: The Disney film, The Lion King, is thought to be loosely based on Sundiata Keita's life.

Sundiata Keita was nicknamed "Lion King" because his name was derived from the word *jata*, which means "lion." Sundiata's father, King *Maghan*, was married to a beautiful woman. His first son was named *Dankaran Touman*. However, the king was told in a prophecy that if he remarried an ugly woman, their son would be the true heir to the kingdom.

When the king's second "ugly" wife gave birth to Sundiata, Maghan was disappointed to find the boy was weak and crippled. He believed the prophecy would not be fulfilled, but he still loved him very much.

The first wife was jealous. She wanted her son to be the king, not Sundiata. She got her wish. When Sundiata was only three years old, his father died. His half-brother, Touman, became king. Touman and his mother were cruel to Sundiata and teased him.

Touman was not in power for long. He was overthrown by the *Sosso people*. Sundiata became a prisoner of the Sosso. As he got older, he grew stronger and began to walk. Once he was old enough, Sundiata fled into exile. While he was away, he became a powerful warrior. Eventually, he was convinced to return home and claim his kingdom.

Sundiata returned with an army and fought a number of battles against the Sosso. He had the support of his people, who were happy to see their prophesized king return. In the *Battle of Kirina*, Sundiata fought against the Sosso leader, *Soumaoro*. Sundiata was victorious. He defeated Soumaoro with a poisoned arrow. With their king gone, the Sosso people were easy to topple, and Sundiata regained his birthright. He then went on to expand the Mali Empire. He named a new city, *Niani*, as its capital.

Fun Fact: Sundiata was the first Mali ruler to use the term *Mansa*, which means "king of kings."

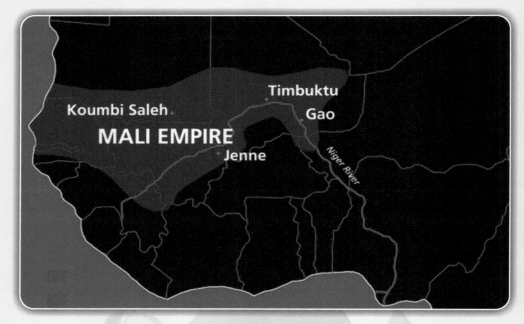

Map of the Mali Empire at its greatest extent.

The Mali Empire was at its most powerful with its ninth ruler, *Mansa Musa*. He was the king from 1312 to 1337. His huge empire spanned across nine modern-day African countries: Mali, Niger, Nigeria, Mauritania, Gambia, Guinea, Burkina Faso, Senegal, and Chad.

Mansa Musa became king because his predecessor went missing! *Muhammad ibn Qu* went on an expedition with two thousand ships to explore the Atlantic Ocean, but he never returned.

When Mansa Musa took over, the Mali Empire was already very rich and powerful. He doubled the empire's land during his rule so that it stretched over two thousand miles. This made it even wealthier, as they gained access to even more trade routes. The three main sources of wealth for the Mali Empire were ivory, gold, and salt.

It is believed that Mansa Musa may have been the richest person of all time! He was so rich that it cannot even be calculated how much he owned.

In 1324, Mansa Musa decided he was going to go on a pilgrimage to Mecca. But as you might expect for the richest man who ever lived, he did it in style. He reportedly traveled there with sixty thousand people, including twelve thousand slaves who catered to his every whim. He also took a caravan of one hundred camels. They each carried three hundred pounds of gold!

Because the gold was so heavy, his camels couldn't carry it past Cairo. So, he gave the sultan of Egypt enormous amounts of gold. He gave away so much gold that the overall value of gold dropped in Egypt. It took twelve years to go back up! This caused widespread economic devastation. Mansa Musa's huge amounts of gold soon meant that the Mali Empire was known all over the world for its impressive wealth.

Mansa Musa was quite literally "on the map." In 1375, a Spanish *cartographer* (mapmaker) created the first European map of West Africa. On it, Mansa Musa was drawn holding a gold nugget and wearing a golden crown.

Mansa Musa brought a number of respected scholars, poets, and architects back home. One of these architects was paid a whopping 440 pounds of gold, which today is worth over eight million dollars! This architect is said to have designed the impressive *Djinguereber Mosque* in Timbuktu.

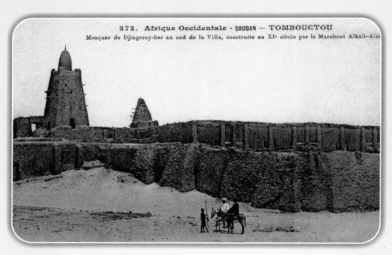

Djinguereber Mosque in Timbuktu
(https://commons.wikimedia.org/wiki/File:Fortier_372_Timbuktu_
Djinguereber_Mosque.jpg#/media/File:Fortier_372_Timbuktu_Djingereber_Mosque.jpg)

Djinguereber Mosque in Timbuktu
(https://commons.wikimedia.org/wiki/File:Fortier_368_Timbuktu_Sankore_
Mosque.jpg#/media/File:Fortier_368_Timbuktu_Sankore_Mosque.jpg)

Mansa Musa also used his great wealth to revitalize the Mali Empire's cities, such as Timbuktu and Gao. Under his rule, Timbuktu became renowned as a cultural center for learning. Its Islamic university became a popular choice for scholars from all over the world to come and study.

Because the Mali Empire was so big, it contained many different cultures and religions. Although Mansa Musa was Muslim, he did not force his religion onto his subjects. He also split the empire into different areas. Each had its own *farba* (governor). They were in charge of keeping the peace in their area and paying taxes and tribute to the Mansa.

After Mansa Musa's death in 1337, the Mali Empire had several different rulers. Many of them contributed to the empire's gradual decline. In 1360, *Mansa Mari Djata II* nearly bankrupted the empire due to his extravagant spending. He did maintain good relationships with Morocco. He even sent a giraffe as a gift for the king! Luckily, Mari Djata II did not live long enough to completely bankrupt the empire. He died in 1374.

In spite of Mari Djata's spending, the empire still continued for many more years under numerous rulers. Over the years, the empire continued to weaken. In the early 1430s, it even lost its famous city of Timbuktu to the *Tuareg*. Timbuktu was then conquered again in 1468 by the Songhai Empire. It had taken one of the Mali Empire's oldest areas of land, *Mema*, three years earlier. The Songhai Empire went on to take over the valuable salt and copper mines from the Mali Empire.

The last ruler of the Mali Empire was *Mansa Mahmud IV*. In 1599, he unsuccessfully tried to take control of the neighboring city of *Djenne*, which had never been part of the Mali Empire before. Unfortunately, he was unable to capture the city. When Mahmud IV died in 1610, his three sons fought over who would take over. None of them ever had full control. Instead, they divided the empire into three, ending the once-great Mali Empire for good.

The Great Mosque of Djenne. Credit: Andy Gilham, Wikimedia Commons.

(https://commons.wikimedia.org/wiki/File:Great_Mosque_of_
Djenn%C3%A9_1.jpg#/media/File:Great_Mosque_of_Djenné_1.jpg)

Chapter 8 Activities

Can you match the Mansa with his achievements?

Mansa Mahmud IV	United the tribes of the Malinké peoples and formed the Mali Empire
Mansa Sundiata Keita	Developed cities like Timbuktu and Gao into important cultural centers and improved the Mali Empire
Mansa Musa	Maintained a good relationship with Morocco
Mansa Mari Djata II	Launched an attack on the city of Djenne that failed

Chapter 8 Answers

Mansa Sundiata Keita	United the tribes of the Malinké peoples and formed the Mali Empire
Mansa Musa	Developed cities like Timbuktu and Gao into important cultural centers and improved the Mali Empire
Mansa Mari Djata II	Maintained a good relationship with Morocco
Mansa Mahmud IV	Launched an attack on the city of Djenne that failed

Chapter 9: Colonization and Enslavement

Toward the end of the Middle Ages, things took a sad turn for Africa and its people. From the 16th century to the 19th century, Africa began to be colonized and enslaved by Western civilizations. Although slavery was still being practiced by the African people, it was less prevalent in the Western world by this point. But even before the official colonization began, Western invaders had been taking slaves back with them. When the Portuguese came in 1442, they began taking African slaves home with them.

However, we tend to think of the transatlantic slave trade as beginning in 1502. This was when the Spanish needed to replace the native slaves in the Caribbean and American colonies. They decided to import slaves from Africa. In 1518, King Charles I of Spain gave permission to the slave traders to directly take African slaves to the Americas instead of having to go through European ports first. This meant that the slave trade began to increase in volume. And there was a great demand for new slaves since the native slaves in the Americas were dying from European diseases and warfare.

The English, Dutch, French, and Danish also began to colonize the West Indies. They decided to replace their existing workforce of poor white people with African slaves.

The first English slave-trading voyage happened in 1562. It was led by *John Hawkins*. The British didn't trade large numbers of slaves until the first English colonies in the Americas were established in the 17th century. During this century, the demand for slaves to work on sugar and tobacco plantations increased, so more slaves were imported.

Book with names, ages, and other details of the slaves
(https://commons.wikimedia.org/wiki/File:Jefferson_slaves.jpg)

By studying the ship logs and manifests that detail the slaves being exported from Africa and sold, historians have been able to estimate that almost twelve million Africans were forcibly removed from their homeland during the transatlantic slave trade. However, as many as 15 to 25 percent of the captured people would not survive the long voyage across the Atlantic Ocean.

More than two million people died on the journey to the Americas due to the dangerous conditions on the boats.

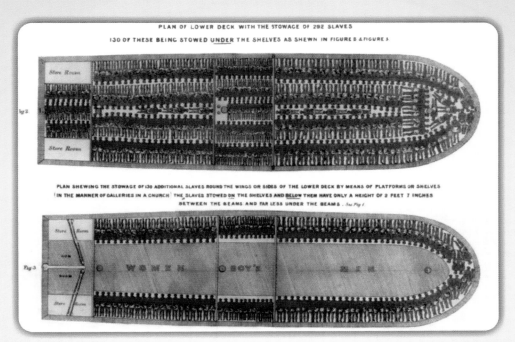

Standard slave ship

The journey across the Atlantic was referred to as *the Middle Passage*. It was about five thousand miles long, which meant it could take several months for ships to reach their destination. The journey was horrific.

The captured African people would be crammed into dirty boats. Men were often chained together so they could not *mutiny* (uprise against the captain). Families would be separated from one another. They were barely allowed up onto the deck to see the sunlight since the crew feared they would uprise.

Below deck, the low ceilings meant they couldn't even sit up straight. Each person had a space of around six feet long, sixteen inches wide, and three feet high. This means they couldn't move or turn over very easily. It was very hot on the ship. Since there were so many people packed on board, there often was not enough oxygen for even candles to stay lit for long.

The length of the journey would often make the difference between life and death. On longer voyages, food would run out. It would then be rationed, with the crew getting priority. Diseases from poor sanitation were also rife.

The ship's crew treated the captured people horrifically. They were very cruel, as they believed that the Africans were less than human. In 1781, the *Zong* suffered problem after problem. Disease spread through the ship, and they encountered bad weather. They were behind schedule, and clean water became an issue. The captain ordered 130 slaves to be thrown overboard to try to save water. Because the slaves were seen as property and not people, he filed an insurance claim for the loss of the money he would have made selling them.

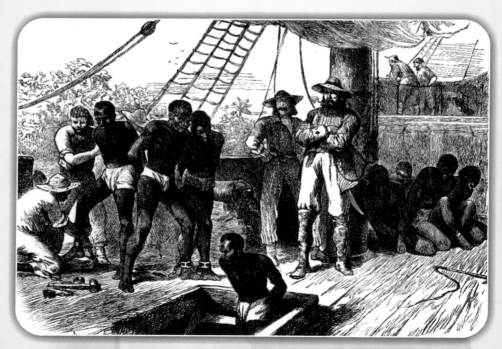

A drawing of slaves on board a ship

Sometimes, the African slaves on ships were able to successfully overthrow the captain. In 1839, a captured slave, *Joseph Cinqué*, led 53 other captives to mutiny against the ship. It was later ordered by the US Supreme Court that the freed slaves should be returned home.

Britain and Portugal were the two biggest slave-trading countries. They were responsible for importing around 70 percent of the slaves. Not everyone in Britain was happy with the slave trade. Some people petitioned for it to be banned for over twenty years before it was finally *abolished* (formally ended). The Slave Trade Act was passed on March 25th, 1807. The United States then followed suit, outlawing the slave trade in 1808.

However, while new slaves could not be imported, owning existing slaves was still permitted. In 1838, the British finally *emancipated* (freed) their 800,000 slaves. Shockingly, in order to free the slaves, the British government also agreed to pay over 26 million dollars in compensation to the plantation owners. The ex-slaves were given nothing for their years of servitude!

It wasn't until 1865 that the United States outlawed slavery. This happened two years after President Abraham Lincoln issued the *Emancipation Proclamation*. The Thirteenth Amendment to the US Constitution abolished slavery, stating that "Neither slavery nor involuntary servitude, except as a punishment for crime whereof the party shall have been duly convicted, shall exist within the United States, or any place subject to their jurisdiction."

The slave trade had a devastating impact on the countries, cultures, and people of Africa. With so many people being forcibly removed (an estimated 25 million between the transatlantic Slave Trade and the

Arabic slave trade), the population and economy of Africa struggled to grow and develop. Because of this, it also paved the way for the colonization of Africa.

HORSE ARTILLERY CROSSING THE DRIFT ON THE MODDER, FEBRUARY 13

A picture of the French cavalry in what is now South Africa
(https://commons.wikimedia.org/wiki/File:French%27s_Cavalry_at_Klip_Drift.jpg)

While foreigners had been coming to Africa for many years, it wasn't until after 1880 that the European colonization of Africa began. Prior to this, most of Africa's interior had been unexplored by Western powers due to disease and difficult travel routes. Ninety percent of Africa was still under African control.

However, in 1884, the *Berlin Conference* was held. It was decided how Africa would be divided among the colonial powers (Britain, France, Belgium, Spain, Portugal, and Germany). Other countries, such as Denmark and the United States, were also involved in the conference, but they went home empty-handed.

Fun Fact: This period is often nicknamed the "Scramble for Africa" since the colonizing powers quite literally scrambled around trying to get their portion of the continent.

There were many reasons why the colonial powers wanted to claim parts of Africa for themselves. Firstly, the more countries under their control, the more powerful they would be. Their power would be known around the world. There was also an economic *depression* going on in Europe. This means the economy was not doing as well as it should. Africa's abundance of natural resources made it an incredibly appealing place to own.

To overcome the big issue of travel, the European colonizers built railways and steamboats that could travel along the African rivers.

The African people did not simply allow invaders to take over their land. They often fought back against Western control. Sadly, most would lose the fight and fall under the control of the invading Europeans. However, Italy was unsuccessful in taking over Ethiopia. The Ethiopians won the fight for their land in 1896.

Fun Fact: The European colonizers wanted to focus on bringing the "three Cs" to Africa: Christianity, commerce, and European civilization.

A Christian revival was under way in Europe. This meant that there were lots of European missionaries who wanted to preach the word of God. They wanted to convert the largely

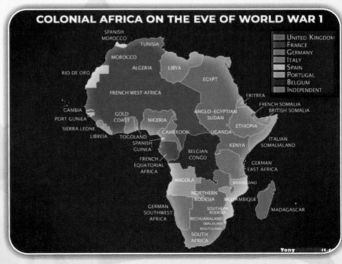

Map of colonized Africa in 1914

Muslim and tribal people of Africa to Christianity.

By the 1900s, a huge portion of Africa had been colonized. The Europeans were able to take control quickly since they took advantage of the rivalries between African leaders. Nature also played a part. In 1895, a severe drought, a plague of locusts, and a cattle plague all meant that there was not enough food. The Africans were too weak to fight back. The invading Europeans also had far better weapons, such as the machine gun. There was also a smallpox *epidemic* (the rapid spread of a disease within a localized region) that wiped out many of the Africans. It did not affect the Europeans as much. They had some *immunity* (resistance to diseases) from previous European epidemics.

The European powers then set about establishing colonial states that were very strict and *authoritarian*. This meant that the African people had no input into how their new colony was run. They also deliberately weakened the indigenous institutions. The colonial powers did not properly fund the colonies, which means there was little in the way of infrastructure.

Fun Fact: The contribution of African people to the war effort during World War I was integral and yet is often ignored.

Chapter 9 Activities

1. Who are the European colonial powers?

2. When did the Slave Trade Act pass? In which country?

3. What happened after the Berlin Conference of 1884?

4. Which amendment ended slavery in the United States?

Chapter 9 Answers

1. Who are the European colonial powers? Britain, France, Belgium, Spain, Portugal, and Germany.

2. When did the Slave Trade Act pass? In which country? 1807 in Britain.

3. What happened after the Berlin Conference of 1884? Africa was divided up between the European colonial powers.

4. Which amendment ended slavery in the United States? The Thirteenth Amendment.

Chapter 10: Decolonization and Independence

During the 20th century, there were many *African independence movements*. These happened when the African people revolted against colonial rule. In 1946, a group of politicians in the French-occupied area of West Africa formed a new political party known as the *African Democratic Rally* or RDA. It played a vital role in the *decolonization* (ending colonialism) of the French Empire.

Meanwhile, in 1948, in British-occupied West Africa, boycotts and riots took place. It was later decided that the African people should have a greater say in government matters with the aim of eventually becoming self-governing nations. In 1951, a new constitution was brought in, and newly elected African leaders became responsible for running the government.

Fun Fact: In 1957 CE, Ghana became the first African country to declare independence from colonial rule.

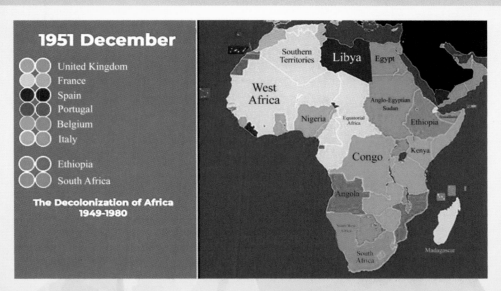

Map of the decolonization of Africa

From 1954 to 1962, *the Algerian War for Independence* took place. The fight for independence from the French had been going on since the First World War. But after the Second World War, the French had still failed to fulfill their promise of giving Algeria more control. So, the *National Liberation Front* began a *guerrilla war* (small and fast movements against military and police forces) against the French. Finally, in 1962, Algeria gained its independence.

In 1963, Kenya also gained its independence from British rule. In the previous decade, there was a massive uprising known as the *Mau Mau Uprising*. The uprising cost the British over seventy million dollars. They were brutal to the Kenyans. They killed civilians and forced many people into concentration camps. The uprising made the British realize things needed to change, and reforms began being introduced. The independence agreement stated that the government would be made up of 66 seats. Thirty-three of those would go to Black Kenyans, twenty would go to other ethnic groups, and the rest to the British.

Fun Fact: The first prime minister of Kenya was *Jomo Kenyatta*, who had been falsely imprisoned by the British following the Mau Mau Uprising.

Although Egypt technically became an independent country in 1922, the British maintained a strong influence over it for many years afterward. Much to the annoyance of the Egyptians, who believed the valuable Suez Canal should be theirs, the British maintained control of it. In 1956, the *Egyptian Nationalist* leader, *Abdel Nasser*, took it from the British and French. This led to a fight for the canal. The British and French were heavily criticized by the United States and other countries for this. Britain was pressured into giving the canal back to Egypt. This was a sure sign that the once-great colonial power of Britain had ended.

South Africa was another country that had a long road to independence. While it technically became independent in 1931, the British *monarch* (king or queen) was still in charge. It wasn't until 1961 that South Africa was declared an independent nation. However, South Africa was still under a racist *apartheid* regime at this time.

Apartheid was a system that favored white people over black people. It enforced *segregation* (the separation of different racial groups. Under apartheid, black people could not own land, own or run a business, or live in certain areas. Marriage or relationships between different races were illegal. Education was skewed. Black students were taught manual skills, and they were unable to attend university. Other laws were introduced that allowed the police to use extreme force and even torture or kill people while on duty. Political uprisings were also strictly monitored. Anyone who seemed to be speaking out would be arrested.

The people still protested, even though it was banned. On March 21st, 1960, a protest against apartheid took place in *Sharpeville*. The police shot into the crowd, and 69 Black South Africans were killed.

Many other countries around the world did not accept the South African regime. It left the British Commonwealth in 1961. It became a republic, but the African people still had no real say. This led civil rights activist *Nelson Mandela* to launch a campaign against apartheid. Mandela's political activism led to him being sentenced to life in prison in 1964. Over the next twenty years, rising pressure from outside countries led South Africa to slowly begin changing its laws from 1986 onward.

Nelson Mandela was released in 1990 after serving 27 years in prison!

On April 26th, 1994, adults from all races were able to vote in elections. A coalition government, with a black majority and Nelson Mandela as the president, came into effect. This date is now known as "Freedom Day" in South Africa. This led to the end of apartheid. However, many racist and separatist ideals still exist in the country today.

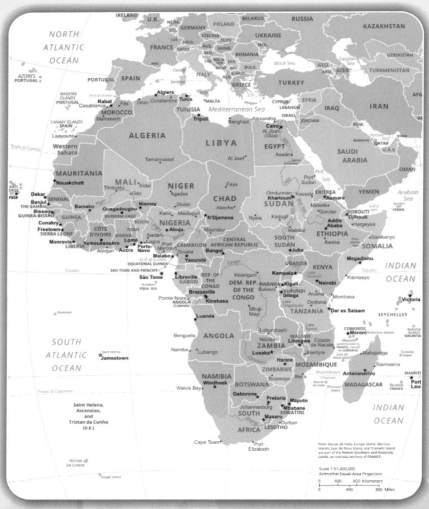

Map of present-day Africa

(https://commons.wikimedia.org/wiki/File:Political_Map_of_Africa.svg)

Nelson Mandela was the first black president of South Africa.

Colonialism and European colonization had a devastating impact on the people and economy of Africa. However, today, Africa is thriving. It has one of the fastest-growing economies in the world. In fact, the overall economy of Africa has gone up by over 400 percent in the past twenty years.

Access to education is improving too. From 2000 to 2020, the number of children attending high school increased by 150 percent!

In the past twenty years, life expectancy in Africa has gone up by almost eleven years!

Africa is also leading the way when it comes to climate change initiatives and green energy, even though it only uses 2 percent of the world's coal. Morocco has built the world's largest solar panel farm. They aim to use 52 percent of renewable energy by 2030. The complex not only provides clean energy for two million people. It also provides jobs for the community. South Africa has introduced a carbon tax that could improve their emissions by 33 percent by 2030. Many other countries in Africa are also introducing similar initiatives.

Now that the African people have control of their homeland, advancements like these will hopefully keep happening, and the continent will continue to thrive.

Can you match the words/phrases to their meaning?

Independence	Formally ended.
Apartheid	Settling of land and controlling the indigenous/native people of an area.
Decolonization	Small and fast movements against military and police forces.
Colonization	The ability for the country to govern and control itself.
Abolish	A system that favored white people over black people and enforced segregation of the races.
Guerilla war	Ending of colonial control.

Chapter 10 Answers

Independence	The ability for the country to govern and control itself.
Apartheid	A system that favored white people over black people and enforced segregation of the races.
Decolonization	Ending of colonial control.
Colonization	Settling of land and controlling the indigenous/native people of an area.
Abolish	Formally ended.
Guerilla war	Small and fast movements against military and police forces.

If you want to learn more about tons of other exciting historical periods, check out our other books!

THE INCA EMPIRE

FOR KIDS

A CAPTIVATING GUIDE TO THE INCAS AND THEIR CIVILIZATION, FROM EARLY BEGINNINGS TO THE SPANISH CONQUEST

CAPTIVATING HISTORY

Bibliography

Want to know more about African history? Check out these books, websites, and videos!

Books:

Kanem-Borno: 1,000 Years of Splendor (The Kingdoms of Africa). Philip Koslow. 1995.

Black History: Kids Edition. Stephen Jones, Sr. 2015.

Who Was Nelson Mandela? Pam Pollack. 2014.

Websites:

https://www.ducksters.com/history/africa/ (Accessed November 2021)

https://www.rebekahgienapp.com/african-history/ (Accessed November 2021)

https://africa.mrdonn.org/ (Accessed November 2021)

Videos:

https://www.youtube.com/watch?v=AlnIdW0pu7o (Created December 2020)

https://www.youtube.com/watch?v=wqRXZJYeRzM (Created April 2016)